A 30-DAY DEVOTIONAL

Walk
with
Me

NUGGETS OF INSPIRATION

LINDA LEE

Walk With Me
Nuggets of Inspiration
by Linda Lee

Copyright ©2017
Distributed by MorningStar Publications, Inc.,
a division of MorningStar Fellowship Church,
375 Star Light Drive, Fort Mill, SC 29715
www.MorningStarMinistries.org
1-800-542-0278

ISBN– 978-1-60708-692-5; 1-60708-692-1

Cover Design: Esther Jun
Book Layout: Michael R. Carter

Dedication

I dedicate this book to every person who reads it. May you be blessed as you read each day's adventure, and may you find your relationship with the Lord enriched with each day's thought.

Acknowledgements

Thank you to my dear friend, Karen Tennis, for the generous gift of computer equipment and the many conversations that spurred me to put on paper what was in my heart.

Thank you, John Boneck, for your encouragement and guidance throughout the process of seeing this book become a reality.

FOREWORD

I have known the power of a spiritual mother's heart.

When I was twelve years old, my father died. My mother was left alone to raise my older brother and me and our four month old sister. Those were tough times. My brother, who could drive, would take me out to have fun on the weekends. When we got home, sometimes in the early morning hours, we would sneak into the house. I can still hear my mother praying for us as we tip-toed past her bedroom door. And I can picture her kneeling beside her bed.

Such is the heart of a spiritual mother.

Linda Lee is one of those spiritual mothers. From an early age, she developed an intimate relationship with the Lord. Now the Father's love comes from her in gentle and touching ways.

When she showed me this daily devotional book, I was amazed at how clear, simple, and yet profound each devotional was. Each was like a friend speaking to me in ways I could understand. They came from the transparent heart of a spiritual mother who has learned wonderful truths.

Whether you are a 50+er like me or you are just starting on life's great road, you will be touched by this devotional's truths. Each devotional takes just a few minutes to read. As you read, let the Holy Spirit speak to you about the day's devotional. He speaks through spiritual mothers and fathers in the Lord—from generation to generation.

John Boneck
50+ pastor, MorningStar Ministries

INTRODUCTION

When deciding what to name this devotional, I had two things in mind. First, I desired that each person reading this book would find their journey with God enriched by His powerful presence each day. Second, in looking into the nature of God and how He interacts with those who love Him, we would increase in love. We can all learn to walk more closely with God and with one another as He deepens our understanding of who He is in and through us, and who we are in Him.

Before the "Fall" Adam and Eve enjoyed daily fellowship with God. He walked with them in the Garden of Eden. Then, because of their disobedience, that fellowship was broken. Only a few, such as Moses, Abraham, and the prophets, could communicate with God. This was the case until Jesus came to earth and restored mankind's ability to once again walk and talk with God the Father.

Jesus told His disciples that after His death and resurrection, the Father would send the Holy Spirit to teach them and guide them into all truth (see John 16:13). Then mankind could communicate directly with God and have divine fellowship with Him once again.

My purpose in writing this devotional is to assist us in keeping our focus on the Lord in this busy and sometimes confusing world. By taking small bites of truth, wisdom, and revelation, we may experience God in our daily lives

The reading plan for this devotional is two-fold:

1) This devotional can be used as a personal journey with the Lord. This five-minute read can last the whole day as it is reflected upon. Each day's reading includes a "ponder thought" or prayer to consider and space to journal thoughts for the day.

2) This devotional can also be used as a discussion guide for group gatherings such as Bible studies, home fellowships, and support groups. Each day's topic and "ponder thought" is a good way to help people open up for discussion.

Thank you for taking this exciting and adventurous walk with me through times of seeking God and finding Him. My prayer is that the reader will be strengthened, inspired, and encouraged to pursue our amazing God—to run after Him with a hunger to know Him more and more.

"When you said, 'Seek My face,' my heart said to You, 'Your face, Lord, I will seek'" (Psalm 27:8).

May the Lord meet us in these times as we invite Him to share our days and direct our steps.

In the Love of Jesus,

Linda Lee

Day
1

HE WILL COMPLETE IT

"Being confident of this very thing, that He who has begun a good work in you will complete it until the day of Jesus Christ" (Philippians 1:6).

This sounds similar to David when he said, **"The Lord will perfect that which concerns me; Your mercy, O Lord, endures forever; do not forsake the works of Your hands" (Psalm 138:7-8).**

The point of both Paul and David above is that God does not expect us to walk this life in our own strength, knowledge, and power. When we receive Jesus into our life, He does not just move on to the next convert and leave us to fend for ourselves. He is committed to accomplishing the things He purposed for us. These Scriptures are powerful reminders of God's love, grace, mercy, and intentions toward those who call Him Lord.

Some of the strongest emotional issues Christian counselors deal with are rejection and abandonment, and the fear of them. Many people carry these feelings from childhood through adulthood and consequently, they never feel adequate to fulfill their calling. They fear failing and not measuring up. When God created us, He knew what He purposed for us and made the commitment to see that come to pass. The problem is, life happens and sometimes causes us to doubt ourselves and God. But that is only a delay. If we will determine to allow God to meet us in that place, we will discover that He is trustworthy.

Let us take hold of these words of comfort and faith, allowing them to fortify confidence in us. Even though we are not yet complete, we can be content in the knowledge that God is with us and will never leave us—and that He will complete what He started in us. Amen!

Ponder Thought: Are you able to receive these words about God as truth and release yourself fully into His hands for the completion of what He started in you? Is it really that easy?

_____

_____

_____

_____

_____

_____

_____

_____

_____

_____

_____

_____

_____

Day 2

ANGST!–OH NO

"Therefore I say to you, do not worry about your life, what you will eat or what you will drink; nor about your body, what you will put on. Is not life more than food and the body more than clothing?

"Look at the birds of the air, for they neither sow nor reap nor gather into barns; yet your heavenly Father feeds them. Are you not of more value than they?

"Which of you by worrying can add one cubit to his stature?" (Matthew 6:25-27).

I remember the first time I heard the word "angst." I was young and thought it sounded like a pretty cool word. I decided to look it up to see what it actually meant. Boy, was that an eye opener. Not everything that looks good (in this case, sounds good), is good. As I read the definition, a somber feeling came over me. Not only did I not know what the word meant, I was acting out that word, and it wasn't a pretty picture!

Angst definition: A strong feeling of being worried or nervous; a feeling of anxiety about your life or situation; apprehension or insecurity.

See what I mean? Not good!

As I read Jesus' words in Matthew, I thought, "This is exactly what He was talking about—not having angst about anything."

Sometimes we bounce along in life thinking what we are doing and saying is pretty cool when it could be the opposite of what we want to be as children of God. Getting caught up in anxiety and worry is so easy to do unless something more powerful captures our attention, like the words of Jesus: "Do not worry!"

Ponder Thought: *Lord, since there is no way worrying will change anything, nor will it help us grow in You, teach me how to trust You more than myself.*

_____

_____

_____

_____

_____

_____

_____

_____

_____

_____

_____

_____

_____

Day 3 — WHOSE PEACE MOTIVATES US?

"Peace I leave with you, My peace I give to you; not as the world gives do I give to you. Let not your heart be troubled, neither let it be afraid" (John 14:27).

Did you ever wonder what the difference is between the peace that Jesus was talking about and the peace the world has to offer? Have you ever had times of turmoil over something (or someone) and then were able to reach some kind of resolution? There is usually a sigh of relief: *"I am glad that is over."* Right? Then it is not long before another situation (or person) pops up, and the whole process starts again. That can be exhausting!

Could the last part of this verse hold the key? Don't let your heart be troubled and don't let it be afraid. I'm thinking that the "let" part is probably an important factor. That seems to put the ball in our court, doesn't it?

A few verses earlier, one of the disciples asked Jesus how He would manifest Himself to them but not to the world. Jesus answered, **"If anyone loves Me, he will keep My word; and My Father will love him, and We will come to him and make Our home with him."** If the Father, Jesus, and the Holy Spirit live within us, a different influence should help us find lasting peace. The world offers temporary fixes based on problem solving and conflict management, but the Lord offers a resolve from within—one that rises up and demonstrates the nature of God based on His humility and love residing within us. We choose how we will respond in situations. Honoring the Lord's presence in our lives will help us find rest in His peace.

Ponder Thought: What makes this so powerful is that the peace Jesus talks about is His gift if we will receive it! If we choose it, there is the promise of the abiding presence of the Lord to help us respond well and maintain the peace He gives us.

Day 4

INTIMATE WORSHIP

"I am my Beloved's, and He is mine!" (Song of Solomon 6:3)

In the quiet of this lovely morning, the thing moving my heart is this thought: **"How excellent is Your name in all the earth" (Psalm 8:1).**

Lord, when I see You in Your magnificent glory before I entertain any other thought, all other things pale to insignificance. When I gaze upon the beauty of who You are and when I see the majesty that surrounds You, my heart is strengthened. My mind is set in confidence that You are a good God and Your love endures forever.

Lord of Glory, how I love You and how I am stirred by the nearness of Your presence. Thank You my King for loving me and making provision for me in all things concerning my life. "I am Yours and You are mine!" You overwhelm me with Your goodness and Your love.

I am very satisfied to sit with You for no other reason than to be with You, and to let You know how much I love You. What joy it must be when Your children come to You without asking for something, pouring out heartaches, or complaining about life and circumstances. Forgive us, Lord, when we forget to just come to love on You and tell You how wonderful You are.

Ponder Thought: Are you able to openly express your love for the Lord? Are you able to sit quietly with Him, not asking for anything but just bringing Him joyous praise and intimate worship? If yes, praise God! If not, ask Him to help you understand why it is uncomfortable. Ask Him to remove any barriers hindering you from coming to Him in pure love and adoration.

He desires that we come to Him in this intimate form of worship even more than we want to be able to come. "And, we are loved by Him, that's who we are!"[1]

_____

_____

_____

_____

_____

_____

_____

_____

_____

_____

_____

_____

_____

---

1   Excerpt from *"You're a Good Good Father"* by HouseFires II. Copyright 2014.

Day
5

NO COMPARISON!

"For we dare not class ourselves or compare ourselves with those who commend themselves. But they, measuring themselves by themselves, and comparing themselves among themselves, are not wise" (II Corinthians 10:12).

It is unwise to let others set our expectations and guidelines because we then measure our success against others. Jesus is the only valid measure for a Christian. Measuring ourselves by any other standard is far beneath where a child of God is called to walk.

In Paul's letter to the Colossians, he said that, **"In Him** (Jesus) **dwells all the fullness of the Godhead bodily; and you are complete in Him" (Colossians 2: 9-10).** If the fullness of everything we need for living life is in Jesus, why would we feel compelled to compare our Christian walk with others?

We each have a unique call from God to walk with Him in the fullness of who He created us to be. We may see someone's walk of faith and be a bit envious, thinking that this is what we want our lives to look like. But wouldn't that be underestimating God's power to bring out in us who He created us to be? May we have the same testimony as the Psalmist who said, **"I will praise You, for I am fearfully and wonderfully made" (Psalm 139:14).** God did not create us haphazardly; He created us with love and purpose.

We see throughout the Scriptures that we are not alone in our insecurities. Many doubted their ability to be who they were created to be. In a letter to the Ephesians, Paul wrote**, "For we are His workmanship, created in Christ Jesus for good works, which God prepared beforehand that we should walk in them" (Ephesians 2:10).** Acknowledging that God created us with a purpose is the first step toward understanding that there is no need to compare ourselves to others, only the need to surrender to Him.

<u>Ponder Thought</u>: *Father, forgive me for not being satisfied with who You created me to be. Show me how to walk in the full measure of my unique calling in You.*

Day 6

ADVANCING THE GOSPEL, EVEN IN ADVERSITY

"Being filled with the fruits of righteousness which are by Jesus Christ, to the glory and praise of God" (Philippians 1:11).

There seems to be adversity everywhere we turn. I'm sure everyone has experienced difficult and challenging circumstances in this life. What is the outcome of these challenging times?

When Paul wrote his letter to the Philippians, he was in prison for preaching the Gospel of Jesus. One thing he wrote about was how everything that happened to him advanced the Gospel of Jesus. Other Christians, and even the palace guards, saw what Paul endured and how he handled it. His conduct while imprisoned was such a strong testimony that it inspired boldness in others to stand up for Jesus, even in the face of persecution.

Whatever the source of the adversity we face, the adversity is not the major issue for a Christian. The issue is how we respond in the adversity. Is the message of Jesus so apparent in our response that it advances the kingdom of heaven and Jesus' message? Is it possible to hold the attitude that the kingdom of heaven moves forward because of how we respond to struggles?

When we are in the middle of a conflict with someone or when a seemingly unfair circumstance stops us in our tracks, we may not consider that we are preaching the message of

Jesus. But isn't that the message Paul spoke? Does our behavior and the things we say when in a difficult situation magnify Jesus? Are we inspiring others by how we deal with challenging circumstances? Food for thought!

Ponder Thought: As I write this, I am reminded of a Scripture that I know we all want to hear some day: **"Well done, good and faithful servant" (see Matthew 25:21).**

THEY, THEM, AND THE ITES

"Be strong and of good courage, do not fear nor be afraid of <u>them</u>; for the Lord your God, He is the One who goes with you. He will not leave you nor forsake you" (Deuteronomy 31:6).

I am curious about "them." You know, the proverbial "they" that are always responsible for whatever it is we try to justify. Oh, maybe that is too cynical—I should probably back up and read more.

It turns out that "them" are all the "ites" that caused Israel so much trouble when they entered the Promised Land. Sorry, I digressed again! I think I should focus on the Lord our God.

God crossed over into the Promised Land before the Israelites. He declared that He would destroy and dispossess "them," and the Lord gave "them" over to the Israelites to deal with according to His commandment. The Scripture above was to be their modus operandi for how to accomplish this commission and inherit the land. The battles had been determined in God's mind, and He instructed the Israelites to be strong, courageous, and not to fear—He would accomplish it all. The Israelites' job was to keep God's instructions and not disobey His battle plan.

Fast forward several thousand years. When asked by the Pharisees which commandment was the most important, Jesus responded, **"Love the Lord with all your heart, soul,**

mind and strength; and the second is love your neighbor as yourself" (Mark 12:31).

So between these Scriptures and also John 3:16, we too are given a modus operandi for securing our eternal home, and also how to keep the commandments God has given us for this day.

<u>**Ponder Thought:**</u> Be encouraged, for "they", "them", and any "ite" you may encounter have already been declared defeated by God on your behalf.

_____

_____

_____

_____

_____

_____

_____

_____

_____

_____

_____

_____

_____

Day

8

Follow Me
and Don't Look Back

"But Jesus said to him, 'No one, having put his hand to the plow, and looking back, is fit for the kingdom of God'" (Luke 9:62).

These words came out of Jesus' conversation with some young men who wanted to travel with Him and be part of His ministry. I don't think there is any doubt that the young men wanted to go with Jesus, but one said, **"Let me first go and bury my father"** (verse 59). Another said, **"Let me first go and bid them farewell who are at my house"** (verse 61). Then Jesus said, **"No one, having put his hand to the plow, and looking back, is fit for the kingdom of God"** (verse 62).

At first glance, Jesus' words may seem harsh to people who believed in Him and wanted to travel with Him. When Jesus said those who looked back were not "fit" for the kingdom of God, He wasn't saying they weren't good enough. Rather, they were not prepared for the serious commitment they would face as they traveled with Him.

Think of a field with rows of newly planted vegetables just beginning to break through the ground. Imagine the beautiful straight rows, but you see a row that is crooked, wandering all over the place. One has to wonder, "Where was that farmer looking when he planted that row?"

When we say to Jesus that we want to be His disciples and serve Him, He could say the same thing to us. We all have things in our past that preoccupy our thoughts and affect our emotions. Paul explained it this way: **"Let us lay aside every weight and the sin which so easily ensnares us, and let us run with endurance the race that is set before us, looking unto Jesus" (Hebrews 12:1-2a).** Did Jesus not say, **"Seek first the kingdom of God and His righteousness" (see Matthew 6:33)?**

Ponder Thought: Focus on where you are going and not on where you have been so that you might be "fit" (prepared, equipped, and ready) for kingdom life.

_____

_____

_____

_____

_____

_____

_____

_____

_____

_____

_____

_____

_____

_____

GRACE UPON GRACE

"And of His fullness we have all received, and grace for grace.

"For the law was given through Moses, but grace and truth came through Jesus Christ" (John 1:16-17).

According to my *Study Bible*,[2] this double term, **"grace for grace,"** means grace piled upon grace. It makes reference to the Israelites in the wilderness. God gave them grace by delivering them from bondage, but they were in need of even more grace to know how to live free and be obedient to God (see Exodus 33:13).

God extended His grace again and again to the Israelites, and Jesus coming to redeem mankind was God's ultimate grace piled upon grace. Jesus not only embodied God's grace, He also embodied the truth and the glory of God in "full measure."

So in my kind of logic, this means that when we accept Jesus as our Lord and Savior, He comes to live within us and grace comes with Him. The more intimate our relationship with the Lord becomes, the more we grow in our understanding of His grace. Every time we meet with the Lord, worship Him, experience His presence, or hear His voice, we experience grace piled upon grace, full of truth and glory (see John 1:14).

---

2 From *The NKJV Study Bible.* Copyright 1997, 2007 by Thomas Nelson, Inc.

I love how Peter described this:

"But may the God of all grace, who called <u>us to His</u> <u>eternal glory by Christ Jesus, after you have suffered a while,</u> <u>perfect, establish, strengthen, and settle you.</u>
"To Him be the glory and the dominion forever and ever. Amen!" (I Peter 5:10-11)

<u>**Ponder Thought:**</u> So now, what are you thinking about that is too hard? What seems unfair? What makes you think God doesn't hear your pleas for help? What is more powerful than grace piled upon grace leading your every step?

_____

_____

_____

_____

_____

_____

_____

_____

_____

_____

_____

GOOD WISDOM OR BAD WISDOM?

"Who is wise and understanding among you?" **(see James 3:13)**

I don't remember ever hearing anyone refer to evil behavior or speech as wisdom. So, I am intrigued with James' comparison of wisdom from above with wisdom NOT from above (see James 3:13-18).

The Apostle Paul said that being carnally minded is against God and cannot please Him. In contrast, being spiritually minded is having a mind set on God and righteousness (see Romans 8:5-8). Look at James' side-by-side view of wisdom (see James 3:13-18):

Wisdom **NOT** From Above (Carnal)	Wisdom from Above (Spiritual)
Bitterness, Envy, Lying, Boasting	Pure, Peaceable, Gentle, Yielding
Self-seeking, Earthly-minded	Merciful, Bearing Good Fruit
Sensual, Demonic, Confusion	No Partiality, No Hypocrisy,
Every Evil Thing	Righteousness

These stark differences are easy to identify. If we read the Genesis account of the Fall (see Genesis 3), we see where earthly wisdom, a kind NOT from above, began.

One definition of wisdom is "An attitude, belief, or course of action." Sad to say, many times the wisdom we display falls under the "wisdom NOT from above" category.

When we receive Jesus, we receive access to "wisdom from above," and the Holy Spirit will teach us to think **"with the mind of Christ" (see I Corinthians 2:16).** But if we choose to continue in our own way of thinking, it will be reflected in our behavior and speech as wisdom NOT from above. We must be intentional about submitting to God, receiving from Him to walk in wisdom from above, for it is found in God.

Ponder Thought: Which wisdom do you walk in—wisdom from above or wisdom NOT from above? *Reveal my heart to me, God.*

Day

11

NEED WISDOM FROM ABOVE? ASK!

"If any of you lacks wisdom, let him ask of God" (James 1:5a)

James spoke of trials as the testing ground for our faith and that we should be joyful when trials come. That doesn't make sense! Trials are not fun!!!!!

This is probably why we have trouble with this trial thing—we are thinking fun while James is nurturing our serious side by talking about the joy on the other side of the trials. James says if we don't know how to walk through trials, we should ask God for wisdom.

While asking for wisdom, we find a lesson on wisdom. We need to ask in faith, without doubting. James called doubting double-mindedness, a wavering back and forth in one's thinking that causes an inability to make sound decisions. Double-mindedness literally means "two souls." If one believes something and is swayed to change and believe another way—and maybe even changes back to the original belief after thinking about it—this is wavering. That mind will be in constant turmoil and confusion, **"unstable in all his ways" (see James 1:8).** That mind cannot receive wisdom, or anything, from God.

We need to be able to make godly choices in a trial. The purpose of trials is not to discredit us or catch us doing wrong, but rather to strengthen and build us up in the character and love of Jesus. This way, we may be established "IN" Jesus, who is our strength, our redeemer, our hope, and our eternal joy.

<u>Ponder Thought</u>: Is there any double-mindedness or doubting within you that is causing conflict in the mind, keeping you from receiving the wisdom of God?

_____

_____

_____

_____

_____

_____

_____

_____

_____

_____

_____

_____

_____

_____

_____

_____

_____

Day
12

FAIR OR UNFAIR?

"Gird up the loins of your mind . . . at the revelation of Jesus Christ" (see I Peter 1:13).

Some may say it is unfair that Christians are persecuted, pressed on, lied about, and challenged at every turn because of their stand for Jesus and the kingdom of heaven. Yet fairness really has nothing to do with it! Fairness would condemn every one of us because of sin. But God's grace and mercy redeemed us and gave us the opportunity to speak about His love and gift of salvation through Jesus. What a privilege to be counted worthy of being targeted by an unbeliever's anger, or to be singled out by the tirades of those who claim they do not believe that there is a God.

Didn't Jesus say, **"If the world hates you, you know that it hated Me before it hated you" (John 15:18)?** Talk about unfair! Jesus was perfect and the world hated Him.

Lord, give us a deeper revelation of Jesus to understand what a blessed people we are, that we are counted worthy of notice by a world that considers us a threat because of our faith and love for Jesus.

Peter said in our lead Scripture, **"Therefore gird up the loins of your mind, be sober and rest your hope fully upon grace . . . at the revelation of Christ Jesus."** In today's vernacular, Peter could have said, "Allow your mind to bear the fruit of resting in the goodness of God to help you speak about Jesus in such a way as to give hope to those who hear you."

I am reminded of stories about the early Christians led to a lion's den or the arenas to fight to the death because of their faith. They sang songs of praise and worshipped God on the way to their deaths. They considered it an honor to die for Christ. Can we count it an honor to live for Christ, even in the face of ridicule?

Ponder Thought: *Father, I pray for Christians around the world being persecuted because of their faith in You. Protect them, Lord, and strengthen them to hold their testimony until the last breath of their lives here in the earth. Amen.* What a reception they will receive in Glory!

_____

_____

_____

_____

_____

_____

_____

_____

_____

_____

_____

Day 13   ABIDE IN HIS HOLINESS

"God said, 'I am holy; you be holy'" (I Peter 1:16, The Message).

I'm thinking this is more than just imitating, or trying our best to be like God. My clue is "be." One definition of "be" is: to exist or have specific characterization, to actually be something, not just look like something (i.e., leaves are not like green; they are green because they are leaves and leaves are green).

Jesus said**, "Abide in Me, and I in you. As the branch cannot bear fruit of itself, unless it abides in the vine, neither can you, unless you abide in Me" (John 15:4).**

There is no way we can be holy on our own. Just like leaves are green because they are attached to the vine, so it must be with us. We have to yield to the holiness of God residing within us. We cannot pick and choose what characteristics of God we would like to display in our lives. Our nature needs to change and make room for God's nature to come forth through us.

In the Fall we see leaves turning color. They are beautiful, but this is their last hurrah before they fall to the ground. The life within the tree stops flowing into the leaves and they soon die. The life within is what makes leaves green. So what looks good is temporary, and its pretty season is short lived.

Wouldn't it be better to stop trying to be holy and just yield to the Holy God residing within us, letting His holiness flow through us all the time?

Ponder Thought: *Teach me, Lord, to let Your life flow through me so that I may live holy in the power of Your holiness. I don't want to just imitate what I think holiness is; I want to be a vessel of holiness that is filled with You.*

TAKE MY YOKE

"Come to Me, all you who labor and are heavy laden, and I will give you rest.

"Take My yoke upon you and learn from Me, for I am gentle and lowly in heart, and you will find rest for your souls. For My yoke is easy and My burden is light" (Matthew 11:28-29).

This is probably one of the most quoted Scriptures in the New Testament. One day, I asked the Lord what being yoked to Him looked like. I immediately saw a vision of myself with Jesus in one of those old, wooden oxen yokes. All I could see at first was our heads in the yoke. We were happy and talking when all of a sudden, the vision opened up to full length. I could see my feet dangling about a foot off the ground. I thought I was walking, but Jesus was actually carrying all the weight.

I was amazed at what I saw and asked the Lord about it. A few days later, I saw the same vision, but this time when it became full length, I could see myself struggling to get my feet on the ground thinking, "I need to carry my part." I went back to the Lord and asked about both visions. The next day, just as with the first two times, I saw it again, only this time my feet were on the ground and I was walking in perfect stride with Jesus. A great deal of peace surrounded us as we walked.

After I saw this third vision, the Lord explained it to me. He said that early in our walk with Him, we do not yet have all we need to walk in faith; He carries us most of that time by the power of His grace. As we grow in faith, we gain confidence and think we can "carry our part," but we still do not have all that we need. Then He explained that we walk in stride with Him when we realize the need for continual relationship with Him. In this place, He guides our every step in every circumstance, and we recognize that we cannot do anything without Him. I remember this vision often and find it an encouraging reminder.

Ponder Thought: What does your walk with Jesus look like? Are you encouraged by what you see?

_____

_____

_____

_____

_____

_____

_____

_____

_____

_____

_____

Day
15

OVERWHELMED
TO OVERCOMER

"**When I am overwhelmed, lead me to the rock that is higher than I**" (Psalm 61:2).

"**Who is he that overcomes the world but he who believes that Jesus is the Son of God**" (I John 5:5).

I recall being in church services where someone gives a compelling message to convince me that I am an "overcomer." I believed the words, but I simply did not feel like I was overcoming anything, let alone everything!

We all face circumstances that seem too overwhelming, making it difficult to see clearly how to overcome. It doesn't necessarily help when someone calls you an overcomer. Knowing these Scriptures does not automatically put us in the feel-like-an-overcomer category.

When we believe in God and in the sacrifice of Jesus, there is the hope and promise that we will come through these times. We overcome by the power of the One who has overcome ALL circumstances for us. He will strengthen and walk with us till we are able to rise above the situation that seems hopeless.

How can we be a source of encouragement to those we encounter, who need to experience the love of God? How can we support fellow believers in overwhelming times? I think of Moses, Aaron, and Hur as Israel battled with the Amalekites. As long as Moses held up his rod, Israel prevailed in battle, but when Moses let his arms down, the Amalekites prevailed. As the battle wore on, Moses became weary and "overwhelmed" with tiredness, becoming too weak to hold up his arms. So Aaron and Hur supported Moses, one on each side. They held up his arms until Israel won the battle against the Amalekites (see Exodus 17:8-16).

<u>Ponder Thought</u>: *Thank You, Lord, for always helping me overcome whatever I face. Show me how to be a genuine encourager for others facing difficulties!*

_____

_____

_____

_____

_____

_____

_____

_____

_____

_____

_____

_____

IN BETWEEN THE "NEVER AGAIN" & "NOT YET"

"For I know the thoughts that I think toward you, says the Lord, thoughts of peace and not of evil, to give you a future and a hope" (Jeremiah 29:11).

As I studied this passage, I thought to myself, *"I wonder why God said that right in the middle of telling the Israelites about being taken captive by Babylon?"* So I backed up to the beginning of the chapter and was blessed by what I discovered.

God gave Israel instructions on what to do when they became captives in a foreign land. First, the Lord made it clear that He was the one who allowed them to be taken captive, and they were the reason it was happening. It was because of their disobedience.

Then God told them His plans for them while they were in Babylon (verses 4-10). He told them 1) to carry on life as normal, 2) to get married, have children, and marry off their children (they were going to be there for seventy years), 3) to seek peace for and pray for the city or place where they would live, and 4) not to be deceived by anyone, including by prophets that He had not sent. After the seventy years, He would bring them back to Israel. By the time I got to verse 11, I could feel the love of God for them. He said that when they turned to Him and prayed, He would hear and answer them (verse 12).

Today, many people feel they are in transition, and it is obvious that we as a country are in transition. Transition is that uncomfortable place where things aren't like they used to be, and it is not yet clear what it will be. It's the "in-between place" that no one really likes. It would be nice if we had some help here! The good news is, God is our help.

Ponder Thought: If we followed the same instructions God gave to Israel, would we find our "in-between" place more tolerable?

_____

_____

_____

_____

_____

_____

_____

_____

_____

_____

_____

_____

_____

_____

_____

_____

Day 17

WHAT AM I CONSIDERING?

"Consider the Apostle and High Priest of our confessions, Christ Jesus" (Hebrews 3:1).

"Looking unto Jesus, the author and finisher of our faith" (Hebrews 12:2).

To consider something is to give it thought in such a way that we come to an appropriate conclusion. In this case, we are to look to Jesus as we consider the matter of faith. Since the Word of God states that Jesus is the author and the finisher of our faith, the appropriate conclusion is the yielding of our will to the will of God. In this way we experience faith. We can trust God to do what He says He would do, and we can believe in His goodness toward us when we trust Him.

Oswald Chambers said in *My Utmost for His Highest*, "All our fret and worry is caused by calculating without God."[3] I think about an unbalanced checkbook—the cause is usually not the bank but a miscalculation on our part. I had to think on that for a few minutes before I got the full impact of what the writer of Hebrews was saying. Finally it clicked. I saw that if we do not consider Jesus first when faced with difficult situations, we will mull it around in our minds. We try to figure out how to make it work when God wants us to consider Him first.

3 Taken from the July 4 devotion. Copyright 1935 by Dodd, Mead & Company. Copyright renewed 1963 by Oswald Chambers Publications Association, LTD.

He has the answers we need. He desires to meet us in those situations and show Himself powerful on our behalf.

I cannot see the words "consider" and "calculate" without remembering these thoughts, and it does cause me to stop and think when I am facing something that requires me to exercise faith. What (or who) am I "considering" to find the answer I need?

Ponder Thought: Are you willing to "reconsider" how you approach situations, relationships, and life to include asking the Lord first what He would have you do?

_____

_____

_____

_____

_____

_____

_____

_____

_____

_____

_____

Day 18

GOD'S DEPOSITS
INTO OUR LIVES

"Put on tender mercies, kindness, humility, meekness, long-suffering;
    bearing with one another, and forgiving one another,
    Let the peace of God rule in your hearts,
    Let the word of Christ dwell in you richly in all wisdom, teaching and admonishing one another . . .
    with grace in your hearts to the Lord.
    And whatever you do in word or deed, do all in the name of the Lord
    Jesus, giving thanks to God the Father through Him"
(see Colossians 3:12-14, 16-17).

While thinking on this Scripture, I sensed the Lord say to me: *"The riches and treasures I pour into you are given to you to hold for Me, to withdraw any time I desire to share with others."* I guess that makes me a depository (like a bank). Now that is a cool thought!

The Lord went on to say:

"My deposits are not meant to be for you alone. They are also treasures you can deposit into others so that they might also become 'depositories for the kingdom of heaven.' The return on those investments and deposits is more than you can think or imagine."

I sensed great pleasure and a smile from the Lord as He said these words. I know this is available to all His children. He is no respecter of persons, and His desire is that we all become rich depositories of His truth, grace, mercy, and love.

Thank You, Lord, for the gracious and powerful trust You place in those who love You and give themselves to You for Your glory. Hold our hearts close to Yours, Lord, so that we may stay in tune with what You are doing. Soften our hearts to be ready at all times to give You our full agreement and participation in sharing with others the treasures You have deposited in us so that we may help in furthering the kingdom of heaven in the earth.

Ponder Thought: *Show me, Lord, what deposits You have made in my life that are not only for my benefit, but for the benefit of those around me.*

_____

_____

_____

_____

_____

_____

_____

_____

_____

_____

A NEW THING

"Do not remember the former things....
"Behold I will do a new thing, now it shall spring forth
. . . I will even make a road in this wilderness and rivers in
the desert" (Isaiah 43:18-19).

There are times in our relationship with God when we feel confident and comfortable. There are also times when we hunger for more and want a new experience in Him. Sometimes we feel like we are "stuck in a dry place." In this place, we are not receiving more and are no longer satisfied where we are. Our comfort level is challenged. New things are usually uncomfortable until they become our new comfort level.

God is faithful to meet us in these places when we declare our trust that He IS doing a new work in us. If we cooperate with Him, God uses these places as a springboard into a new revelation of who He is and who we are in Him. We may expect God to use what we already know and have experienced to take us to a deeper place, and He may do that. Yet He may also want to establish a new revelation from a deeper deep, a higher high, and a wider wide than we have experienced.

In this Scripture, God says He will make a new road and supply rivers in the dry places. One reason we sometime feel stuck is because we expect the new to be an extension of the old. After all, the old was not bad. But this may be a time when He is saying He wants to do a brand new thing, one created by Him alone.

God told the Israelites not to remember the former things. They had been held in bondage in former times and were not prepared for the new thing God was doing. They did not yet have a reference point for the new, except for God's faithfulness. That is exactly what He extends to us in the new things—His faithfulness!

Ponder Thought: *Thank You, Lord, for what You have done in me up to this point. Now help me see the new You have prepared for me. Help me cooperate with You in establishing the new in me to the glory of God.*

Day 20 — THIS LITTLE LIGHT OF MINE

"You are the light of the world...
"and it gives light to all who are in the house. Let your light so shine before men . . . and glorify your Father in heaven" (Matthew 5:14-15).

I can't tell you how often I recall the little songs I learned in Sunday school. I usually remember all the words and the fun hand motions that went with the song. They got into my head and I'd sing them for days. I guess that is the point—to remember the message. "This Little Light of Mine" was one such a song. I can attest to the Scripture, **"Train up a child . . . he will not depart from it" (see Proverbs 22:16).**

When I moved into my new home a few years ago, I put my trusty little nightlight in the bathroom and was thankful for a lighted path for the middle-of-the-night trip in new surroundings. The problem was, I couldn't go back to sleep because the light seemed like a floodlight. So, I got up and followed the lighted path back to the bathroom and turned it off, thinking I wouldn't need it the rest of the night. On my way back to bed, I banged my knee on a chair. Then I stubbed my toe on the bedframe. Boy, did that hurt!

The next night, I turned the light on but closed the door so it wouldn't be so bright. I climbed into bed and couldn't believe it—it was brighter than the night before! Not only could I see the light in the bathroom, it was reflecting in a mirror. Now there were two lights! This battle went on for a few nights until I accepted that I needed the light. I had better adjust to it and be thankful for it.

I know this doesn't sound like a spiritual story, but there are several spiritual markers in it. I pray that the Lord will reveal what He wants each of us to glean from this story.

Ponder Thought: Are you battling with the light or are you a source of light that reflects the nature of Jesus?

_____

_____

_____

_____

_____

_____

_____

_____

_____

_____

_____

_____

_____

Day 21

MORE THAN, BIGGER THAN, GREATER THAN!

"Blessed is that man who makes the Lord his trust" (see Psalm 40:4).

"I will put my trust in Him" (see Hebrews 2:13).

When we place our trust in God—even when that trust is small—it is amazing how God gets us right where He purposed we should be. We spend our lives thinking we make our own choices about what is best for our lives only to find out it is really God's unseen hand that accomplishes His will and unfolds our destinies.

What was it like for Noah, Moses, Abraham, John, Paul, and others to walk with God, hear His voice, and see evidence of His involvement in their lives? As born-again believers, we can have the same experience with God, only better. We have the advantage of the Holy Spirit's presence and guidance living within us. He teaches us all things and leads us into all truth as we seek to walk as Jesus taught His disciples to walk.

Part of trusting God means believing His greatness is bigger than anything else we can see or know. He is the One who created all things, and the name of Jesus is above every name. When our current need looms before our eyes, we can see ourselves as "grasshoppers" as the Israelites did when they were preparing to enter the Promised Land. Thank God for Joshua and Caleb who saw God and themselves as "more than, bigger than, and greater than." We have this promise to hold onto in

times of need: **"For with God nothing will be impossible"**
(Luke 1:37).

Another part of trusting God is bypassing what we think or
see, going straight to the truth of God and holding on to that
truth for dear life UNTIL we see that truth come to pass. Don't
become fainthearted while waiting. God is more than enough
for our need. His word is truth and He will bring it to pass.

Ponder Thought: **"Lord, I believe, help my unbelief!" (see**
Mark 9:24)

_____

_____

_____

_____

_____

_____

_____

_____

_____

_____

_____

_____

_____

_____

Day 22 — Unexplainable Comfort

"For the Lord comforted His people" (see Isaiah 49:13).

"Your rod and Your staff, they comfort me" (see Psalm 23:4).

"God of all comfort who comforts us . . . that we may be able to comfort others" (see II Corinthians 1:3-4).

God is able to comfort a nation and an individual at the same time. What an amazing and compassionate God we serve!

It is impossible to live life and not experience the need for comfort. Even the most mature Christian faces times of trial, fear, disappointment, and grief. God's intimate knowledge of His creation recognizes that and provides perfect comfort for any circumstance. God is perfect in all His ways (see Psalm 18:30). God not only comforts us, but He also calls us to comfort others as we have experienced His love, grace, compassion, and comfort.

The power of comfort is not that it changes circumstances, but rather that God does not leave us to face circumstances alone. There is no emotional upheaval, no startling news, no tragic happening we can experience that is more powerful than the hand of God touching His beloved children in those times. That knowledge in itself is a tremendous comfort.

You may say, "I don't agree because the grief I have over the loss of my loved one cannot be comforted." I understand that feeling and have experienced it firsthand. Yet the truth is, God created us, and only He knows what our grief really feels like. As hard as it may be, we are the ones who choose whether or not we will receive comfort. When we choose to receive all God extends to us, an unexplainable Divine thing happens that shifts the weight of our sorrow and our grief into the arms of God. **"He heals the brokenhearted and binds up their wounds" (Psalm 147:3).**

Ponder Thought: *Help me, Lord, to receive Your comfort and be ready to extend that same comfort when I meet someone who needs it.*

_____

_____

_____

_____

_____

_____

_____

_____

_____

_____

_____

_____

DIDN'T OUR HEARTS BURN?

"Didn't we feel on fire as He conversed with us on the road, as He opened up the scriptures for us?" (Luke 24:32, The Message)

One of today's "Christianese" phrases is, "send Your fire, Lord." Who has not said that because we want more and more of God? I wonder, though, what would happen if He showed up in holy fire right beside us? I would venture to say we would drop to the floor with our faces to the ground. Isn't that what happened again and again in the Scriptures?

I have, as you may have, been in church services when the Spirit of the Lord descended. There was a powerful change in the atmosphere, and people received healing, instant deliverance, and hilarious joy. I love it when this happens, but I also love it when the Holy Spirit shows up in my personal prayer time. All of a sudden, the tears begin to flow. I fall to my knees, and it feels like I can't breath. I don't want to move because I don't want His holy presence to leave. An awesome fear causes me to want nothing more than to please my God and King. During those times, I am compelled to examine my heart before Him and ask Him to burn out anything not pleasing and glorifying to Him.

When Jesus walked with the two men on the road to Emmaus, He asked them what they were discussing. They told Him what had happened in Jerusalem and about the death of

Jesus, not realizing they were talking with Jesus. He explained the Scriptures that told of His life and all that would happen, and they were so stirred in their hearts they didn't want Him to leave. So He ate with them, and when He broke the bread, their eyes were opened and they saw it was Jesus.

As exciting as the manifestations of His presence are, how much more life-changing is it when His fire burns within us, revealing Himself and aligning us with His heart?

Ponder Thought: *May I walk with You, Lord, until I know Your fiery presence!*

_____

_____

_____

_____

_____

_____

_____

_____

_____

_____

_____

_____

Day
24

SEEING THE UNSEEN

"So we fix our eyes <u>not</u> on what is seen, but on what is unseen. For what is seen is temporary, but what is unseen is eternal" (II Corinthians 4:18).

When we look at what is in front of us, we have a couple of choices. We can allow what we see to discourage us to the point of giving up, or we can choose to allow the inner eyes of our faith to see God. He intervenes on our behalf, giving us confidence that through Him we will prevail. When we look only at what is seen, we leave God out of the picture.

The word "*look*"[4] in the verse above means "to keep one's eyes on" or to "concentrate on." We cannot help but see what we see, but we can determine how long we will "look" at it, and how long we will "concentrate" on it.

A perfect example of this is the story of Elisha and his servant in II Kings 6. I suggest reading the whole chapter. Syria was at war with Israel, and the King of Syria sent his army to find Elisha and bring him back to give counsel to the King. The Syrian army surrounded Elisha's camp, and when Elisha's servant saw the army, he was afraid. Elisha told the servant not to be afraid because there were more with them than there were with the army. Then Elisha asked God to open his servant's eyes. He did, and the servant saw a host of angels in fiery chariots surrounding the army. Is that amazing, or what?

---

4 Definition taken from *The NKJV Study Bible.* Copyright 1997, 2007 by Thomas Nelson, Inc.

I'm not saying that we will have visions of angels in fiery chariots every time we are in difficult circumstances. I am suggesting that we not concentrate on what we see, believing it to be more powerful than God's ability to deliver us. **"If God is for us, who can be against us?"** (see Romans 8:31)

Ponder Thought: May we be aware of what we look at and be ready to envision our God meeting us in that place to help us. **"Son of man, look with your eyes and hear with your ears, and fix your mind on everything I show you"** (see Ezekiel 40:4).

_____

_____

_____

_____

_____

_____

_____

_____

_____

_____

_____

_____

_____

Day

25

SHHH! JUST WAIT!

"The Lord is good to those who wait for Him...it is good that one should hope and wait quietly" (Lamentations 3:18).

You might say, "Waiting I understand, but why do I have to do it quietly?" Have you ever shared something in a "private conversation" only to have someone (or several someones) ask you about that very thing later? Sometimes it seems that interested parties monitor our life circumstances, with ready suggestions and opinions on what we should do and how we should do it.

However, when the Lord gives us a direction, an assignment, or tells us something He is about to do, it is a good thing to follow this Scripture's advice and hold it quietly before the Lord in hope. Wait for His timing.

When it takes a long time for a thing to come to pass, it is easy to grumble. If we are not careful, we can step into murmuring. There is always someone who will help us murmur, and I'm thinking this may be part of the delay in seeing the fulfillment. We do not want to start doubting that we heard the Lord, or even worse, accusing the Lord of not fulfilling what He said He would do.

The instruction to wait quietly is for our own benefit, to help us stand in faith until we see a thing come to pass. We can't receive a thing through boasting or whining or even discussing it with others, so it is best to wait quietly for God's unfolding of it.

A good example of this is David's life. Even though it took years, he didn't gloat or talk about when he would finally be able to become king. Joseph is another example. He spent several years in prison before his promise was realized. Joseph's waiting resulted in God's blessing upon his family and the whole nation of Israel.

Ponder Thought: Are you waiting on something from the Lord? Could it be that waiting is part of the testing of your faith on the matter?

Lord, help me have confidence in my relationship with You. Help me to quietly wait and trust You.

_____

_____

_____

_____

_____

_____

_____

_____

_____

_____

_____

THOUGHT LIFE

"Let the words of my mouth and the meditation of my heart be acceptable in Your sight, O Lord, my strength and my Redeemer" (Psalm 19:14).

This is the last verse in a "Psalm of Wisdom." David wrote this to honor God for who He is, for His creation, and for the purity of His Word. David ends the Psalm with this prayer of submission of his thought-life to God.

Have you ever heard that it is better to think a thing than to say it? I understand this sentiment, but it doesn't quite line up with this Scripture, does it? We can sometimes get caught off guard and find ourselves accidently saying what we are thinking, only to embarrass ourselves and others. Of course, we cannot take the words back after they are spoken. Perhaps we should take David's guidance and look deeper at our thought patterns.

Paul spoke of this as being part of our arsenal in spiritual warfare: **"pulling down strongholds, casting down arguments . . . bringing every thought into captivity to the obedience of Christ" (see II Corinthians 10:3-6).** This is not just something we do in prayer for others—we should first apply it to our own thoughts and words. Rather than looking at this as a series of dos and don'ts for warfare, this is the power of disciplining our thought lives before the Lord. In doing so, our words, thoughts, and consequent actions give place to God, not to the enemy of righteousness.

When our normal pattern of thinking is monitored by our desire to please God, we are more likely to speak in a way that encourages, edifies, and builds up those we encounter in day-to-day conversations.

Ponder Thought: *Lord, may the words of my mouth reflect my willingness to submit my heart and my thoughts to You. My desire is to honor You and glorify Your name in all things, at all times.*

_____

_____

_____

_____

_____

_____

_____

_____

_____

_____

_____

_____

_____

_____

NURTURING CONTENTMENT

"Now godliness with contentment is great gain" (I Timothy 6:6).

Sometimes to understand the impact of a statement, it helps to look at the reverse of what is said. In this case, ungodliness can cause discontentment, or discontentment can cause ungodliness. I don't think any reasonable Christian would sign up for either of these. When we allow ourselves to practice ungodliness or discontentment, we fall prey to the enemy of our soul who wants to steer us away from God. In such a case, trying to function in godly faith would be impossible because we do not always put our hope and belief in something that is God. Sometimes we place our faith in a system, or most often, in our own abilities and desires.

Paul the Apostle must have wrestled with this because in his letter to the Philippians he said, **"I have learned in whatever state I am, to be content" (see Philippians 4:11).** In our opening Scripture, Paul was passing this lesson on to Timothy to encourage him in his mission at Ephesus.

An important thing in our walk of faith is learning how to trust God in all circumstances, and rest in His goodness toward us. It is not always easy to trust, but isn't that the point? If things were easy, why would we need God's help? Nothing about walking in faith is easy in our own knowledge and understanding; otherwise Jesus would not have had to be sacrificed on our behalf. If left to ourselves to find contentment, it most surely would lead to ungodliness for we would seek pleasures to meet our idea of contentment. Praise God for His word and for those who have learned and share valuable lessons of faith, godliness, and contentment.

<u>Ponder Thought:</u> Are godliness and contentment evident in your life? Is it of great gain, or is it more of a hit-and-miss, once-in-awhile thing?

Help me, Lord, as I learn to find lasting contentment in You.

Day 28 — THE GIFT OF DISCERNMENT

"Those by reason of use (practice) **have their senses exercised to discern good and evil"** (Hebrews 5:13-14).

During the Charismatic Renewal movement, I began to hear the word *discernment* in connection with the Christian life. As a child, I was taught godly principles of right and wrong and how to make choices based on that understanding. Yet this discernment thing was different. I'm sorry to say, there was quite a bit of immaturity during that learning curve of Spirit-filled living that led to many people seeing a devil in everything and everyone. But, praise God for His grace and mercy when Christians learn new things.

It became apparent to me that the power of discernment was not to be used to validate one's gifting, or to recognize something wrong, unspiritual, or an evil spirit. The redeeming power of discernment lies in the ability of a child of God to recognize when to speak words of life, hope, and love. This opens gates of bondage to set the captive free to the glory of God. As our opening Scripture says, the more we practice submitting our discernment to the Lord, the more sensitive that discernment becomes in recognizing the difference in good and evil.

The difference is that in immaturity, one can recognize something that is morally or spiritually wrong but then concentrate on their ability to remedy the problem. The focus should not be on our own insights. The focus should be on the one who needs to see Jesus and be redeemed by His power, authority, and love. The more we spend time learning from the Holy Spirit how to discern good from evil and what is in the heart of God, the richer the gift of love we have to offer the one in need.

Ponder Thought: *I come humbly before You, Lord, asking You to renew my ability to discern good from evil, to use it for Your glory.*

_____

_____

_____

_____

_____

_____

_____

_____

_____

_____

_____

_____

_____

Day 29

HAVE I TOLD YOU LATELY THAT I LOVE YOU?

"He has brought me to His banqueting place, and His banner over me is love [waving overhead to protect and comfort me]" (Song of Solomon 2:4, Amplified).

A few months after I married my husband, Larry, out of nowhere he starts singing to me, "Have I told you lately that I love you? Well darlin', I'm telling you now." I laughed and cried at the same time because it touched my heart. For those of you not old enough to know, this song, "Have I Told You Lately that I Love You," was written in 1945 by Scotty Wiseman and recorded by many country music artists of that era. All Larry could remember were these two lines, but it was enough for me to get the message that he wanted me to feel special, and I did. This happened frequently throughout our thirty-seven years together. Shortly before he passed away, he did not have the energy to sing those words, but he said them to me and it warmed my heart, as it always did.

Shortly after Larry passed away, the Lord said to me that He was now my husband. He would take care of me and I should rest in Him. What comfort those words were in my grief. A few days later, I spontaneously sang those words to the Lord. I can't imagine the delight the Lord must have felt with one of His hurting children singing those words to Him. I did this often with the Lord, and one morning I heard His voice saying, "I love you more!" I was undone and felt such assurance of His presence with me every moment of every day. God's love and gentle comfort brought me through that grief period, and

I continue to this day with an occasional rendition of that song during my devotional time with Him.

"Have I told you lately that I love you? Could I tell you once again somehow? Have I said with all my heart and soul how I adore you? Well, darlin', I'm telling you now " (verse one).

Ponder Thought: God knows our hearts, and He knows how to draw us near and give us peace, comfort, and love when we need it. Can we do less than tell Him how much we love and adore Him?

_____

_____

_____

_____

_____

_____

_____

_____

_____

_____

_____

_____

FINALLY!

"Finally my brethren, be strong in the Lord and in the power of His might" (Ephesians 6:10).

As I read this verse, I sensed the need to think about the implication of these words. It was the word *finally* that stopped me. Paul's letter to the Ephesians is full of rich spiritual insight for living in relationship and walking in maturity and victory. Then He sums it up by shining the spotlight on the power to accomplish it all—God Himself!

Even when we listen to and read good sermons by powerful men and women of God, and when we put into practice what we learn, it boils down to our submission to the power and might of God, and our trust in Him to secure the victory in and through us. When we acknowledge the Lord in every circumstance, we see, hear, and know the blessings of walking with a God, our total provision in all things. He teaches us by His Spirit of Truth, and He equips us by His mighty hand, fortifying us for part of His glorious army. In the midst of this, He brings peace to our minds and rest to our hearts.

Paul's admonition to **"be strong in the Lord"** reveals a powerful truth for a believer in Jesus Christ. When we grow in the power and might of God, we learn to rely more on His strength, power, and might than on our own. God is the provider, Jesus is the victor, and we have been invited to be a part of it all. God does not need us to accomplish anything, but He desires that we be by His side to reap the fullness of every victory. The Lord is our "finally" for everything, including our eternity. Praise His name forever!

Ponder Thought: *You alone are God most holy, and I worship You in spirit and in truth. Thank You, Lord, for loving me and being my everything!*

_____

_____

_____

_____

_____

_____

_____

_____

_____

_____

_____

_____

_____

_____

_____

_____

PUTTING IT ALL TOGETHER

Now that you have completed these thirty days of focus on the Lord, what is the most significant thing(s) the Lord revealed about Himself to you through these daily devotions? Use the space below to record what the Lord has shown you about His nature during this time, and list any significant things that may have surprised you and brought joy to your daily walk with Him.

_____

_____

_____

_____

_____

_____

_____

_____

_____

_____

_____

_____

_____

_____

_____

_____

_____

Walk With Me